D1518358

UNCOVERING
AMERICAN HISTORY™

A PRIMARY SOURCE INVESTIGATION OF
THE SALEM
WITCH TRIALS

ZOE LOWERY AND
JENNIFER MACBAIN-STEPHENS

rosen publishing's
rosen
central

Published in 2016 by The Rosen Publishing Group, Inc.
29 East 21st Street, New York, NY 10010

Copyright © 2016 by The Rosen Publishing Group, Inc.

First Edition

Library of Congress Cataloging-in-Publication Data

Lowery, Zoe, author.
A primary source investigation of the Salem witch trials/Zoe Lowery and
Jennifer MacBain-Stephens.
     pages cm —(Uncovering American history)
Includes bibliographical references and index.
ISBN 978-1-4994-3513-9 (library bound)
1. Trials (Witchcraft)—Massachusetts—Salem—Juvenile literature. I.
MacBain, Jenny, author. II. Title.
KFM2478.8.W5L69 2015
345.744'50288—dc23

                                                        2014044552

Manufactured in the United States of America

CONTENTS

I t seemed as if the hysteria would never end. The residents of Salem Village, Massachusetts, were so traumatized by the events of the witch hunts that even sixty years after they ended, the residents wanted to distance themselves from the horror. So they changed their town name to Danvers. In part, the community wanted to stop sharing taxes with the town of Salem Town—now known simply as Salem—but it's widely known that the witch trials were not discussed openly for years.

In February 1692, Samuel Parris's nine-year-old daughter, Betty, and her eleven-year-old cousin, Abigail Williams (who had been orphaned and lived at the Parris home), began exhibiting strange behavior. When Parris returned home from work one day, he found the girls contorting themselves in impossible positions, cowering under chairs, sticking out their tongues, and screaming gibberish. Lacking any natural explanation, Parris's physician, Dr. William Griggs, decided that the girls were "bewitched."

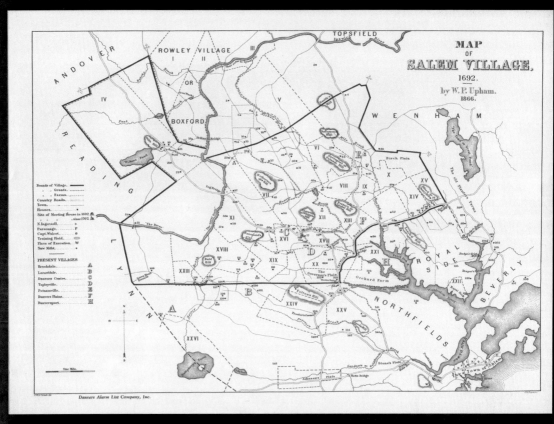

In 1692, about 600 people built roughly ninety houses on 20 square miles (52 square kilometers) of the marshy Salem Village, as shown on this 1866 map designed by W. P. Upham.

Back in 1692, Salem—its residents trying to get settled in this new community isolated in the wilderness—was about to face a horrific year.

CHAPTER ONE

A NEW BEGINNING GOES WRONG

The Pilgrims escaped religious persecution in 1620 and set up a new community in America. Within twelve years, twenty thousand immigrants had settled in their new home and the Puritans settled in Massachusetts in 1630. The Pilgrims were seeking to completely separate from the religious laws of the Church of England. The Puritans, who believed that every human being was predestined to enter either heaven or hell, had plans to reform, or purify, these doctrines.

In 1620, the Pilgrims settled in Plymouth, about 50 miles (80 kilometers) south of what became Salem, where wealthy Puritan merchants created the Massachusetts Bay Colony. Nine years later, the Puritans set up their own government and laws, as had the Pilgrims.

In 1672, the governing body of Massachusetts, the General Court, gave the men of Salem Village—the farming section of Salem—permission to lay plans for a meetinghouse. In 1689, Reverend Samuel Parris was elected as minister. By examining various documents, historians have discovered that Parris was an extremely stern man who was obsessed with the idea of sin and his own self-importance. His wife, Elizabeth, was very sickly and was often confined to her bed. Because Parris was often away on church business, his family was frequently left alone.

By 1692, the area of Salem—which consisted of the prosperous Salem Town and Salem Village—had more than six hundred residents. There was tension between the town and the farming village. The agricultural community wanted to govern themselves instead of having to rely on the financial support of the town. The farmers felt that the town was becoming too modern and that Puritan values were not being upheld.

In the seventeenth century, under British law, colonists found to have been consorting with witches or the devil were guilty of having committed a felony. This felony was punishable by hanging. On February 29, 1692, the first arrest warrants were issued for three women whom the "bewitched" girls claimed had afflicted them. About two hundred more arrests were made in the coming months by different people. In May, pressured into putting an end to the madness, Governor William Phipps set up the Special Court of Oyer and Terminer (to "hear and determine"), which was finally dissolved in October when the trials came to an end.

HARD TIMES

Salem Village was radically different back in 1692 than today (present-day Danvers and most of Middletown and Peabody, Massachusetts). The people of Salem Village did not have an easy life. They were constantly dealing with political upheaval from England, attacks from Native Americans, and land wars. In addition, the climate was quite

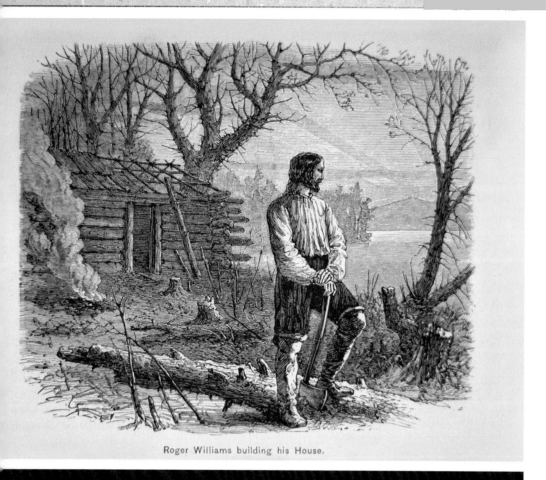

Roger Williams building his House.

Pastor and teacher Roger Williams arrived in Massachusetts in 1631, but by 1635 he was banished to Rhode Island (shown here) when his views contradicted those of the General Court.

harsh, and there was always a threat of smallpox outbreaks. Meanwhile, immigrants were pouring into this up-and-coming trading post. Conservative Puritans felt threatened by these outsiders. Adult Puritans were instructed to be devout and tranquil, and so were their children, who were required to behave likewise. Play was considered lazy and was strictly forbidden.

ACCUSED!

Possibly in an attempt to escape this rigid lifestyle, nine-year-old Betty Parris and eleven-year-old Abigail Williams—who were often joined by a small group of girls—secretly played fortune-telling games. In one game, the girls would ask questions about the future and then drop an egg white into a glass of water to see what shape it took. One February night in 1692, Betty saw a picture of a coffin, and suddenly her body began to contort into odd shapes and

The witchcraft scare probably started with voodoo stories West Indian slave Tituba told Betty Parris and Abigail Williams and their friends. The girls soon claimed they were possessed and blamed Tituba.

she started screaming. One of Parris's servants, John Indian, baked a "witch cake," a mixture of rye meal and the girl's urine, in an attempt to find out who was torturing her. John Indian would then feed this cake to the Parris's dog, and if it acted strangely, the adults could determine whether or not the girls were indeed bewitched.

The two girls accused three women of witchcraft, all of whom lived in what is now known as Danvers Central: Tituba, a slave who was in her twenties, thirty-nine-year-old Sarah Good, and forty-nine-year-old Sarah Osbourne. Sarah Good was a beggar woman. Sarah Osbourne had a "questionable" past: she had married her Irish manservant, Alexander Osbourne, and was thought to be somewhat unintelligent.

 ## MOTIVES?

Perhaps Sarah Good and Sarah Osbourne were targeted as witches because they had bad reputations in the community. Tituba was the girls' caregiver and was constantly in their presence. For other accused persons, it might have been personal politics that sent them to their deaths. Some historians believe that Ann Putnam Jr. was acting on the behalf of her parents, Thomas and Ann Sr., who had many motives (as we will see later on) for wanting to get rid of certain individuals. No matter what her motives were, Ann Putnam Jr. was responsible for the imprisonment and eventual hanging of many innocent people.

The accused were first "examined" by judges John Hathorne and Jonathan Corwin at the Salem Village meetinghouse. The "examinations" consisted of harsh questioning. According to Frances Hill in *A Delusion of Satan*, a judge would bully and scream at an accused and terrified person, "What familiarity have you with the devil?" Then there would be invasive and surely humiliating probing to discover a "witch's mark." A mark could be anything from a pinprick to a freckle to a birthmark.

ACCUSATIONS OF ANN

Shortly after Abigail Williams and Betty Parris accused these women, twelve-year-old Ann Putnam Jr., seventeen-year-old Mary Walcott, and seventeen-year-old Elizabeth Hubbard (the niece of Dr. William Griggs, who had labeled Abigail and Betty "bewitched") also began to exhibit "fits," and they, too, accused a slew of people. It is possible that Ann, who lived only a mile away, or Mary Walcott, who lived only a few hundred yards from Betty and Abigail, also joined in on the fortune-telling games.

According to some accounts, these girls formed a spiritual circle, or a coven, to try to foretell their futures. Young Ann became a sort of ringleader of the group, accusing the most people of witchcraft, including four-year-old Dorcas Good. It is possible that these girls half believed that they really were being "afflicted" by witches.

CHAPTER TWO

FUEL FOR A FAMILY FEUD

To understand the grave situation in Salem in 1692, it may be helpful to examine the life of Betty Parris's father, Reverend Samuel Parris. Reverend Parris lived in the Salem Village parsonage after the departure of Reverend George Burroughs, who was later accused of witchcraft. Parris's father, Thomas Parris, had an estate in Barbados, and when Thomas passed away, the younger Parris went there to settle the affairs of the sugar plantation. When Parris left the island in 1680, he took two slaves with him: Tituba and John Indian. He moved to Boston and soon married Elizabeth Eldridge. In 1686, Parris began substituting for absent ministers, and he campaigned to be the new Salem Village preacher.

The Putnam family handpicked Parris to be their new minister. The influential Putnams owned the most farmland in Salem Village, and they used their wealth to establish their own church congregation. They opposed the modern ways of Salem Town and wanted to separate from it. More than half of the village congregation were Putnams. The Putnams paid Parris a small salary and provided him with firewood. He also received money from local taxes. But Reverend Parris also got several extra bonuses from the Putnam family.

Parris was also able to obtain the title and deed to the parsonage and the surrounding land. This newfound ownership gave him stability and power. This was a rare transaction for the time period.

In October 1691, a new Salem Village committee was assembled. The committee, mostly made up of opponents of Parris from Salem Village, refused to pay the local tax. They also questioned his ownership of the ministry house. He feared he would lose his position. Parris made sermons about how evil was taking over Salem Village and how there were conspiracies by the devil at work. With Parris losing money (taxes paid his salary), the Putnams feared they would lose him and the formation of a new community that the congregation brought.

When Betty Parris and Abigail Williams had fits, Parris called on his powerful friends to hold prayer meetings and days of fasting, hoping these things would rid the girls of evil. He supposedly beat his servant Tituba into confessing. Tituba's life was spared only because she had confessed out of terror.

As for the other women who were accused, the

Although Reverend Samuel Parris was specifically chosen to be the new minister in Salem Village, this man of God was not immune from the accusations of witchcraft.

proceedings against Sarah Good were particularly cruel since falsehoods were discovered as the trial was going on. One girl cried out that Good's apparition was stabbing her with a knife. Upon examination, a broken knife was found on the girl. Sarah Good stayed in jail for months and was finally sentenced on June 29, 1692. She was hanged on July 19. Sarah Osbourne would never set foot outside prison walls again; she died in prison on May 10, 1692. Throughout 1692, hundreds of people were accused of witchcraft. The magistrates of the Massachusetts Bay Colony began preparations to question the accused.

CURIOUS COURTROOM CONFESSIONS

The private questioning and examinations in quiet rooms gave way to public courtroom dramas. At these trials, more than forty people confessed to being witches. In some cases, those confessing accused others. It is not surprising that people were not emotionally or intellectually equipped to defend themselves against the bullying judges. Ironically, those who confessed were often let go, and those who proclaimed they were innocent Christians ended up going to jail or being hanged.

HEIGHTENING HYSTERIA

When the governor of Salem, Sir William Phipps, set foot on Massachusetts soil with his minister friend and president of Harvard, Increase Mather, in mid-May 1692, accusations of sorcery were flying, examinations were under way, and people were already awaiting further trials. This was an important visit, however, because Mather brought with him

HERE COMES THE JUDGE: WILLIAM STOUGHTON

William Stoughton lived from 1631 to 1701. He was appointed the chief magistrate over the Court of Oyer and Terminer (the special court that heard the witch trials). Although he was certainly very well educated, having received a degree in theology from Harvard University and an M.A. from Oxford University, Stoughton had a shocking lack of any legal education or training whatsoever. Under Stoughton, procedures in the courtroom deviated from the norm: He tolerated private discussions between the judges and the accusers, and he forbade any defense for the accused. Despite his role in perpetuating the trials, Stoughton suffered little political damage after the hysteria died down.

the colony's new charter. The previous charter proclaimed that instead of being a self-governing body, the colony had to be ruled by a governor from England. But that charter had expired at the end of 1689 when the English king, James II, was overthrown. The colony had been without a valid government for two years. It was during this time that witchcraft mania began. Before any laws from this new charter could be put into effect, Phipps watched as hysteria grew in Salem. He felt that he had to take action.

According to *A Delusion of Satan*, Phipps wrote in his diary: "When I first arrived I found this province [most] miserably harassed with a most horrible witchcraft or possession of devils."

As an emergency measure, Phipps set up the Court of Oyer and Terminer. William Stoughton, a friend of William Phipps's, was very excited to take his new post: chief magistrate. Born in 1631, Stoughton possessed an ongoing interest in government. Stoughton is remembered for his role in the trials as being one of the most relentless judges of his time. Historians tend to discuss him at length because he admitted spectral evidence into the courtroom, which was very effective in prosecuting people. Puritans believed that witches could send out their specters, or shapes, from the inside of their bodies. These specters had human powers of sight, hearing, and touch, and could transport themselves out of prison cells or fly through the air at will.

After the prestigious Special Court of Oyer and Terminer (made up of seven judges) was established, it was not long

BOLD BRIDGET BISHOP

The first woman to be hanged in Salem was Bridget Bishop. Bishop was the first accused witch sentenced for execution by the Court of Oyer and Terminer. On occasion, Bishop wore a bodice with the color red woven through it. The community considered this manner of dress inappropriate. In addition to having been married three times, Bishop also ran a tavern at her house, and she was accused of drinking apple cider all night. Also, she was previously accused of witchcraft years earlier and was known for quarreling with her husband in public, which was against the law. Ten years earlier, Bishop had been forced to stand back-to-back, bound and gagged in the center of town with her husband, Thomas Oliver, because they had quarreled in public. When Bishop was accused of witchcraft, there was no one to come to her defense: Bishop didn't have any powerful friends.

Bridget Bishop was accused of witchcraft for reasons including weaving red into her clothes and arguing with her husband, which was illegal. This memorial seat commemorates her unfortunate death.

before someone suffered from its judgment. On June 10, 1692, Bridget Bishop (fifty-two years old) became the first "witch" to be hanged on Gallows Hill. The afflicted girls had never met Bishop, but they knew her by reputation. Bishop had been taken to court twelve years earlier on a witchcraft charge. Though she had been found innocent, there remained rumors of her activities.

Fifty-year-old wife and mother Deliverance Hobbs had apparently been watching the trials with keen interest. On June 2, 1692, she claimed at the trial that Bishop had wanted her to "sign the Devil's book or she would whip her with iron rods." (Later, Hobbs's own daughter Abigail accused her of witchcraft. She flatly denied any wrongdoing at first, but—perhaps because of the ruthless methods of questioning—she eventually confessed to just about any charge anyone mentioned.) More and more people from the town came forward to testify against Bishop. Samuel Gray declared that she had killed his child fourteen years earlier, a claim he would admit was a complete lie as he lay dying. First thing in the morning on June 10, Bishop was carted from the Salem jail, along Prison Lane, to Essex Street, out of town to Boston Road, and then to be hanged on a tree on the steep, rocky hill known as Gallows Hill.

CHAPTER THREE

OUTRAGEOUS ACCUSATIONS AND OVERFLOWING PRISONS

According to some historians, seventy-one-year-old Rebecca Nurse was so ill that authorities likely had to pull the ailing woman right out of bed to arrest her on March 23, 1692. In spite of her claims of innocence, Nurse had

Tompkins Harrison Matteson's *Examination of a Witch* is thought to depict examinations during the Salem witch trials, complete with Mary Fisher being stripped to look for the devil's mark.

to be "examined" by judges Hathorne and Corwin in addition to two physical examinations by midwives.

Midwives were often used in examinations to search the bodies of the accused for a mark. The mark could be a freckle or something completely normal. Since the Puritan dress code was so conservative, it is unreasonable to think that villagers could even determine what an "abnormal" mark would be. They obviously did not have practice seeing one another unclothed. In some cases, midwives might come to completely different conclusions, which meant the accused would have to endure still a third examination.

REBECCA NURSE

Rebecca Nurse was the perfect image of Puritan piety. If someone like her could be accused of witchcraft, then no one in Salem was safe. Rebecca Nurse, born in 1621, was the daughter of William Towne and Joanna Blessing. She had two sisters, Mary Easty, fifty-eight—also put to death for witchcraft—and Sarah Cloyce, fifty-one, who, though she was accused, escaped death. Nurse's seventy-four-year-old husband, Francis, made wooden trays for a living and was well liked in the community.

According to historians, it is possible that Nurse—an upstanding citizen—was targeted because she and her husband had recently come into a large amount of land and the townspeople were envious of her acquisition. The story behind this coveted land is that in 1678, Francis Nurse had begun renting a large plot of land that included a farmhouse. Because he was hardworking, he would eventually be able to buy the property. It's also possible that the envy toward the Nurses resulted from the fact that Francis had risen politically in their hometown of Topsfield. According to historical documents, the city of Topsfield had been in a dispute over its border with Salem Village. The Putnams owned the land on the Salem side. The Putnam family estate was also on this tract of land. The townspeople's suspicions of Rebecca Nurse made them equally doubtful of her husband. To make matters worse, although Rebecca Nurse was strongly affiliated with the church in Salem Town, Francis was an outspoken critic of Reverend Samuel Parris and his sermons.

Local gossip suggested that Rebecca's mother had been accused of witchcraft years earlier, although she had never been tried. And people believed witchcraft was passed down from mother to daughter. It is possible that all these factors contributed to Rebecca

Rebecca and Francis Nurse were a model Salem couple. When they took over their house (shown here) and property, they made improvements, which may have made some townspeople jealous.

Nurse's eventual condemnation. Proof of her unblemished reputation was evident when many people, who had perhaps kept silent before, came forward to speak for her innocence. Still, her accusers focused only on Rebecca's mother's past, and hence charges were brought against her.

IN CHAINS: WAITING IN PRISON

When any citizen made complaints against supposed witches, they were required to come before the magistrates for preliminary hearings. When the magistrates felt that there was enough evidence for a trial, the accused was put in jail and had to wait for a hearing before a grand jury.

At the time, people felt that if the witches were chained up, they had less chance of releasing their specters out to attack people. Often, they were placed in ankle-to-neck chains. Once the witches were locked up, the town waited to see if the girls' fits would cease. When they did not, there were other arrests and examinations. While Nurse was being examined, middle-aged community member Elizabeth Proctor was denounced as a witch on March 28, and one of Nurse's sisters, Sarah Cloyce, was accused on April 3. John Proctor, age sixty, was also accused and imprisoned.

When the accused were not being examined, they waited in prison, and soon enough the prisons began to fill up. On April 19, 1692, while Rebecca Nurse stood chained, Abigail Hobbs, the twenty-two-year-old daughter of Deliverance and William Hobbs, Giles Corey, age eighty, and Mary Warren, age twenty, were being examined. Three days later, nine more people were examined. Among this group was Nurse's other sister, Mary Easty. It was not surprising that families and spouses of the accused were arrested because townspeople also believed that witchcraft was contagious. After the examinations, which could last anywhere from three to five days, the accused returned to prison.

Because the jails were usually far away in Boston or Ipswich, a visit to the accused meant leaving the farm untended for a long period of time. If new mothers were in jail, they did not know if their babies were getting milk. Author Frances Hill, in *A Delusion of Satan*, describes the

Salem jails as "places not just of privation but of horror. As the most dangerous inmates, the witches were kept in dungeons. They reeked of unwashed human bodies and excrement. They enclosed as much agony as anywhere human beings have lived. Since they were so close to the banks of the tidal river, they were probably infested with water rats . . . [The prisoners'] limbs were weighted down and their movements restricted by manacles chained to the walls."

One may understand why someone like Sarah Good, who had no money or connections, was accused, but why would anyone accuse someone like Rebecca Nurse? Nurse was the first of the "unlikely" witches to be accused. Nurse confessed: "I am clear. For my life now lies

This document begins the transcript of the execution of Rebecca Nurse, who was executed on July 19, 1692. Before she died she begged God to forgive her accusers. (For a transcription, see page 51.)

in your hands." Nurse's family immediately tried to secure her reprieve. When Governor Phipps granted her one, the accusers once again had fits and the community concluded that this was proof enough that she was guilty.

Nurse was sentenced to death on June 29 and executed on July 19. On the scaffold, she asked God to forgive those who accused her.

MEMORIAL

It was not until 1711 that the government compensated Nurse's family for her wrongful death. Her body had been thrown into a shallow grave on a rocky hill near the execution site. Her family came back late at night and took her body back to their home for a proper burial. In 1885, Nurse's relatives erected a memorial to Rebecca. Finally, in 1992, the remains of another accused witch–or wizard, as a male witch was called–George Jacobs Sr., age eighty, was also laid to rest in the Nurse family plot.

The Rebecca Nurse Homestead in Danvers, Massachusetts, includes 27 acres (11 hectares) of fields, pasture, and woods. This property, cared for by the Homestead Preservation Society, is owned by the Danvers Alarm List Company, Inc. Today, the house includes three restored rooms with period furnishings from the seventeenth and eighteenth centuries. A short distance away on the grounds is a reproduction of the 1672 Salem Village meetinghouse. The meetinghouse was usually where the witches were "examined" by magistrates. Though the plaque states that Nurse died on June 19, she actually died on July 19, 1692.

SKEPTICAL IN SALEM

Nurse's hanging seemed to increase a sense of skepticism among the townspeople. As more and more people were being accused, the atmosphere in Salem was filled with doom: neighbors watched neighbors sit in jail while their homes fell into decay and disrepair.

There was a lot of bad feeling surrounding Nurse's death. Widespread skepticism resulted in a backlash against Reverend Samuel Parris. The anti-Parris group would see their heyday. As the trials wore on, Parris continued to preach his stern brand of Puritanism, constantly voicing the vital need to wash away sin. Two years after the trials had run their course, in 1694, Parris was an unpopular individual in Salem. According to *A Delusion of Satan*, Parris said, "Everybody points at me, and speaks of me as by far the most afflicted minister in all New England." Parris finally admitted that he might have been a bit wrong in playing a part in the trials. Regardless of his seeming change of heart, his apology was not accepted. His enemies, those who did not take communion at his church—the elderly Samuel Nurse, Peter Cloyce, John Tarbell, and Thomas Wilkins— were determined to remove him from the parish.

Parris apologized for his actions on November 26, 1694, reading a statement to the congregation in the meetinghouse. He and his family stayed in Salem Village until September 1697. After the new anti-Parris committee in the village paid him for the parsonage deed, he moved his family to Stowe, Massachusetts. Parris died in 1720.

CHAPTER FOUR

ACCUSATIONS, TRIALS, AND TESTS

Unfortunately, hundreds of men and women were accused of witchcraft before Samuel Parris finally left Salem. Soon the girls were not just accusing community outcasts; the most influential people in the community—the rich and powerful—were called out, too. But when the girls called out Mrs. Margaret Thatcher—none other than the magistrate Jonathan Corwin's mother-in-law—matters started to spin out of control.

In 1692, Judge Corwin was fifty-one years old. He was a member of one of the most prominent families in Salem. The afflicted girls also accused two sons of former governor Simon Bradstreet and the wife of Reverend John Hale. Eventually, in October, the girls accused Lady Phipps, the wife of Sir William Phipps, their appointed governor from England who had set up the court in the first place. However, none of these society figures were arrested.

The Salem judges were unrelenting in their persecution of individuals. Judge Corwin ignored pleas and letters to end the trials, and Judge Hathorne continued the practice of using the words of the

The "witch house" was the home of magistrate Jonathan Corwin and is the last standing structure directly linked to the trials. Today it houses the Salem Witch House Museum.

accused against them by bullying them and manipulating their statements.

Judge Hathorne was an extremely religious man. Because of his beliefs in the supernatural, he took accusations of witchcraft very seriously. Hathorne was known for acting more like a prosecutor than an impartial judge. Hathorne died, unrepentant, on May 10, 1717. Author Frances Hill notes in *A Delusion of Satan*: "Hathorne's only comeuppance has been an extremely unflattering character portrayal as Judge Pyncheon in Nathaniel Hawthorne's *The House of Seven Gables*. Alas, the novel was

Nathaniel Hawthorne, shown here, portrayed the real-life Judge Johnathan Hathorne as the brutal, unmoving Judge Pyncheon in his novel *The House of the Seven Gables.*

written a hundred years after Hathorne's death so he never saw himself vividly pictured as a cruel, rigid tyrant. Perhaps sometimes in the small hours he sweated with fear at the possibility that he had caused twenty innocent people to die."

The film *The Crucible*, directed by Nicholas Hytner in 1996, is based on the famous play by Arthur Miller. In the play, the Salem judges—Hathorne and Corwin—are depicted as evil. Miller's drama is still popular today. In March 2002, *The Crucible* opened on Broadway in New York City's Virginia Theater. According to historians, the young "afflicted" girls may have been very skilled liars who were responsible for many deaths. However, it's also possible that they believed in their own afflictions.

In Increase Mather's "Memorable Providences Relating to Witchcraft and Possessions: A Faithful Account," he made note of one afflicted girl: "In November following, her tongue for many hours together was drawn like a semicircle up to the roof of her mouth, not to be removed, though some tried with their fingers to

THE WITCH-LESS WITCH HOUSE

The "witch house," as it is known locally, was built in the early 1670s. It is located at the intersection of Essex and North Streets in present-day Danvers, Massachusetts, and it was the home of magistrate Jonathan Corwin. When he was twenty-four years old, Corwin purchased the home from Nathaniel Davenport.

In spite of its name, no person ever accused of witchcraft either lived or was imprisoned there. This is the only structure still standing with direct ties to the Salem witch trials. In 1944, the house was nearly destroyed when the city wanted to widen North and Essex Streets. Concerned citizens got together to save the historic home, and the organization called Historic Salem Incorporated was born. Demolition was prevented.

Author Enders Robinson describes Corwin in *The Devil Discovered: Salem Witchcraft*: "Corwin's father had settled in Salem in 1638. He had accumulated a fortune, serving in the upper levels of the colony's government. Through fortuitous marriages, the Corwins were allied with the most notable families of Massachusetts. When he was thirty-five, Jonathan Corwin married thirty-one-year-old Elizabeth (Sheafe) Gibbs, a widow who had inherited a great fortune." Corwin is buried near his house, in the Broad Street Cemetery.

do it. Six men were scarce able to hold her in some of her fits."

Some judges and ministers wrote down accounts of what they saw and would then use these diary entries as evidence in court. Some other writings that were used to prosecute Bridget Bishop were Sir Matthew Hale's "Trial of Witches" (1662) and Richard Bernard's "Guide to Jurymen" (1627). In addition to reading what acts of evil witches could be guilty of (including appearing barebreasted or pinpricking someone), there were also judges' "tests."

One such test concerned the Lord's Prayer: if it could be recited without making a mistake, the person was definitely not a witch. (It was thought that Satan would not allow his followers to recite the prayer correctly.) Another sign of being a witch was a witness's testimony of the accused having supernatural strength. If a poppet—a small doll made of rags and hogs' bristles—was discovered, this was considered hard evidence against the accused (even though there was never any proof that poppets were used to perform dark deeds).

Ann Putnam Jr. accused sixty-two people by the time the witch hunt was over, and any remaining people in jail were let go in May 1693. Perhaps she really believed at the time that someone or something from the dark New England woods was torturing her. Years later, both of her parents died, leaving her to raise her nine brothers and sisters on her own. Ann, however, did something that none of the other girls in the "circle" did. She publicly acknowledged her role in the witch trials. In 1706, she stood before the church as her pastor read her apology:

I desire to be humbled before God for that sad and humbling providence that befell my

A scene from the Salem witch trials is expressed in a woodcut engraving (artist unknown). A woman defends herself to the judge as an "afflicted" girl writhes on the floor.

father's family in the year 1692. That I, then being in my childhood, should by such a providence of God, be made an instrument for the accusing of several persons of a grievous crime, whereby their lives were taken away from them, whom now I have just grounds and good reason to believe they were innocent persons; and that it was a great delusion of Satan that deceived me in that sad time, whereby I justly fear that I have been instrumental, with others, though ignorantly and unwilling to bring upon my self and this land the guilt of innocent blood.

Some of the other girls who made accusations of witchcraft against their innocent Salem community members—Elizabeth Booth, Sarah Churchill, and Mary Walcott—finally got married and left Salem behind. As for seventeen-year-old Elizabeth Hubbard or twenty-year-old Mary Warren, history comes up blank. Abigail Williams may have gone insane, based on the word of historian Sir Matthew Hale.

CHAPTER FIVE

TOADS, TEMPERS, AND THE MATTER OF THE MATHERS

W omen were hardly the only ones to shoulder harsh accusations of witchcraft during the Salem witch trials. Men from every background also had to face Salem's magistrates and defend themselves from all sorts of accusations.

GEORGE BURROUGHS AND THE TROUBLE WITH TOADS

Formerly a pastor in Salem Village, George Burroughs had a long history of disagreements with the Putnams. Burroughs had graduated from Harvard and was known for his physical strength as well as his intellect. He had also traveled extensively. It is possible that his worldliness was a threat to the Putnams.

Before living in the Salem parsonage in 1681, Burroughs spent nine months living with John Putnam Sr. and Putnam's wife. Through diary accounts, historians have pieced together that there had been tensions in the Putnam house and, ultimately, Burroughs moved into the parsonage in 1681. By 1683, his salary payments had stopped. Jonathan Putnam may have rallied supporters to drive Burroughs away. Because he was not getting paid, Burroughs left the parsonage, and the congregation was without a minister. Then, the town threatened to sue Burroughs, who had fled to the town of Casco, Maine. Eventually, he returned to settle his affairs. Putnam wanted to arrest Burroughs, but

A hand-colored woodcut shows the execution of George Burroughs, who was accused of leading all the witches. Condemning evidence included toads in his home. Toads were considered the devil's tools.

because Burroughs had made other friends in the town, six villagers came to his defense and he ended up receiving the salary that Putnam had withheld from him. Burroughs then happily returned to Casco.

Nine years later, field marshal John Partridge took a shocked George Burroughs from his dinner table in Wells, Maine, and accused him of witchcraft. Partridge delivered Burroughs to the Salem magistrates on May 4. In questioning Burroughs, judges discovered he did not take communion, and he admitted there were toads in his new home. According to the judges, toads were instruments of the devil. Twenty-two-year-old Abigail Hobbs and eighteen-year-old Mercy Lewis testified that Burroughs was not only a wizard but also the leader of all the witches.

When Burroughs was thrown in prison, thirty-two people signed a petition on behalf of his innocence. However, it was of no use. Burroughs was hanged on August 19, 1692. Standing in front of the crowd, waiting to be hanged, he stunned everyone by reciting the Lord's Prayer perfectly and quickly. Some people called out for his pardon, but the judges refused to hear their pleas. Twenty years later, the government gave his children a monetary compensation for their father's wrongful death.

THE TEMPER OF GEORGE JACOBS

George Jacobs was born in England in 1617. Jacobs was not as well respected as George Burroughs. Not only did Jacobs attend church infrequently (a definite strike against him), he was also known for his temper and crude language. He was outspoken, cranky, and easily enraged. The Puritan community did not think very highly of Jacobs's outbursts. All of these shortcomings could indicate a possible reason for his having been targeted for the trials.

Tompkins Harrison Matteson's 1885 painting depicts George Jacobs's trial. Jacobs's fiery temper and irregular church attendance were infamous in the community and may have led to his guilty verdict.

He was condemned for practicing witchcraft the first week in August 1692. When he could not properly recite the Lord's Prayer, he was found guilty of witchcraft. Jacobs is reported in Frances Hill's *A Delusion of Satan* as having said, "Well burn or hang me. I'll stand in the truth of Christ." When he was hanged with George Burroughs on Gallows Hill on August 19, 1962, he protested, "I am falsely accused. I never did it."

Immediately after the execution, the sheriff and his officers went to Jacobs's house and seized everything the family owned, including his wife's wedding ring. After

Jacobs was hanged, his family secretly buried him on their own land. In 1864, some of his descendants who were still living on the land unearthed his skeleton—possibly while farming or remodeling the buildings. His remains were taken to Salem in 1992 and reburied as part of a ceremony marking the 300th anniversary of the trials.

A man who perhaps expressed guilt about the hangings, Samuel Sewall was forty years old when he served on the Court of Oyer and Terminer. Sewall was the only judge who

THE PERILS OF PERIWIGS

Judge Samuel Sewall, who lived from 1652 to 1730, was born in Hampshire, England, and settled in the Massachusetts Bay Colony in 1661. In 1671, he graduated from Harvard. Before his career in government began, he married into wealth when he and Hannah Hull were wed in 1676. Friends with Governor Phipps, he was appointed to the Court of Oyer and Terminer in 1692.

Later in his life, Sewall became known as a famous diarist (one who keeps a diary and then publishes it). He constantly wrote in his diary about the "horror" of the "periwigs" that he had to wear during the trials. A periwig is the fake white hair that British magistrates traditionally wore in court and that is still worn today. He graduated from Harvard and wrote a controversial piece called *The Selling of Joseph* (1700), which was one of the first publications against slavery.

ever apologized for his role in the Salem trials, though he had a reputation that would have suggested otherwise—he was known for reducing his children to tears by constantly reminding them of death. In January 1697, Sewall surprised everyone: he handed in a paper at the assembly of the (new) General Court in Boston that stated that he wanted "to take the blame and shame of the opening of the late Commission of Oyer and Terminer at Salem." As recorded in Sewall's diary, he asked that God "not visit the sin of him, or any other, upon himself of any of his, nor upon the land." The new government was happy that such shameful events were over. The whole experience was regretted, certainly, but no one wanted to take the blame.

THE SERMON THAT CHANGED SALEM

Though Salem was a small isolated city, outside influences began to infiltrate the troubled town. Two of these influences were Increase and Cotton Mather.

Increase Mather and his son, Cotton, were members of the elite in the colonies. They made names for themselves by documenting several sensational court cases, as well as writing their own philosophies on parenting, morals, and religion. Increase was the son of a wealthy minister who had come to Massachusetts in 1635. (In those days, it was very popular to give children unusual or religious names, such as Reform, More Mercy, Restore, Believe, and Tremble.) Increase, born four years after his father had entered the colony, was given his name, according to Frances Hill in *A Delusion of Satan*, "because of the never-to-be forgotten increase, of every sort, wherewith God had favoured the country."

Although believers in witches and witchcraft, father and son—both of whom were ministers—were eventually in favor of stopping the executions in Massachusetts. Increase eventually wrote a famous piece that questioned the use of spectral evidence. It was called "Cases of Conscience Concerning evil Spirits Personating Men, Witchcrafts, infallible Proofs of Guilt in such as are accused with that Crime," and it was published in 1693. (It was based on a sermon he preached on October 3, 1692.) This famous piece was published near the time that Increase's own wife was named as a witch, but no charges were brought against her.

Increase Mather's "Cases of Conscience" caused the course of the Salem trials to be rerouted. Mather wrote, "It were better that ten suspected witches should escape, than that one innocent person should be condemned." This work was first delivered as a sermon to a group of ministers in Cambridge, Massachusetts, on October 3, 1692. It cast serious doubts on the use of spectral evidence. Why these judges took so long to doubt the use of spectral evidence in court remains a mystery. At this time these men and their friends were all being accused of witchcraft, so researchers believe this may have swayed their views.

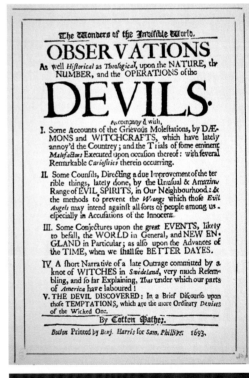

Cotton Mather and his father, Increase, were famous for their sermons and pamphlets such as this one. Eventually they endeavored to cease the execution of witches in Salem.

CHAPTER SIX

PITILESS PRISONS AND PUNISHMENTS

The judges were apparently unaware of the conditions in the prisons. Had they known, they probably would have been shocked and horrified. When the Court of Oyer and Terminer was finally dismissed on October 29, 1692, forty-nine people still suffered in jail. Sarah Osbourne, Roger Toothaker, an unnamed infant of Sarah Good's, Ann Foster, and Lydia Dustin had all died while in prison.

YOUNG AND OLD ALIKE

The thought of innocent people locked up in a wretched jail is horrible, but even more chilling is the fact that Dorcas Good, a small four-year-old girl, was locked up for eight months. Her mother, Sarah, had already been executed. Dorcas spent her days chained to the wall, able to move only her fingers. Prison wardens probably paid no attention to her, thinking she was the devil's servant. When Dorcas was finally released from the prison, her health had been so severely compromised that her father had to pay a keeper to look after her until she died. She had gone mad.

Some doctors believe that in certain psychological conditions, such as abuse or neglect, a strong desire to hurt or even kill is established. Researchers Carol F. Karlsen, in *A Devil in the Shape of a Woman*, and Frances Hill, in *A Delusion of Satan*, noted that in accusing Dorcas—the child of an outcast who had no one to speak for her—perhaps the afflicted girls were acting out an impulse that comes from having been over-controlled or unloved.

It wasn't enough that people were suffering in prisons and being hanged from trees. Although hanging was the usual punishment for those convicted of practicing witchcraft, other gruesome deaths took place in Salem during the climax of the witch

This 1692 petition for bail from the accused witches describes the wretched conditions in the Boston prison. They were often chained to the wall, even children like four-year-old Dorcas Good. (For a transcription, see page 51.)

hunt. On September 19, 1692, Giles Corey, age eighty, was stripped naked, a board was placed upon his chest, and then, while neighbors watched, heavy stones were placed on top of the board. It took two days for him to die. Supposedly, near the end, Corey's tongue came out of his mouth and the sheriff pushed it back inside with his cane. The only words that Corey said were, "More weight, more weight."

Trial of Giles Corey.

This illustration depicts the trial of Giles Corey, who stoutly refused to plead guilty or innocent and was thus the only man to be pressed to death.

Ann Putnam Jr., Abigail Williams, and Mercy Lewis accused this prosperous farmer of witchcraft. Ann Putnam claimed the specter of Corey visited her on April 13, 1692, and asked her to write in the devil's book. Later, she also said that a ghost appeared to her and told her that Corey had murdered him.

Corey was examined and then forced to stay in jail with his wife for five months while he awaited trial. When he was brought into the courtroom, there was a flurry of "evidence" against him. One witness announced that she had seen Corey serving bread and wine at a witch's sacrament.

Corey was quite certain that he would be convicted. Spurred on by his hopeless situation, he did something shocking: he refused to stand trial. He also pointed out to

CRUSHED

Giles Corey was the only man to have been pressed to death because he refused to enter a plea. (Throughout the trials, close to two hundred men and women were accused.) One theory as to why Corey refused to say whether he was innocent or guilty is that by avoiding a conviction, it became more likely that his farm, which he had just deeded to his two sons-in-law, would not become property of the state after he died.

Corey might have been accused because he was friends with those who supported Israel Porter, a powerful anti-Putnam member of the community. Corey was a devout member of the church, but he had a bit of a tainted past. He was known to quarrel with his wife, Martha, whom he helped send to prison when charges were brought up against her. Corey had been brought to court in 1675 for possibly having beaten a manservant to death.

the judges that no one really escaped the Court of Oyer and Terminer.

On his court date, Corey's silence caused the magistrates to order "peine forte et dure," or "strong and hard punishment." Prisoners who would not make a plea faced pressing, an old English punishment. The idea behind pressing was that the victim would finally say something. This brutal punishment had never been used in New England before, and this was the first and last time it was used.

CHAPTER SEVEN

AN END IN SIGHT

Sir William Phipps created a new court that did not consider spectral evidence and convicted few defendants. Phipps pardoned the remaining defendants as well as others awaiting execution.

The Court of Oyer and Terminer was finally terminated in October 1692. Increase Mather's famous sermon changed public opinion about spectral evidence forever. When an afflicted girl named his wife, Governor Phipps decided he had finally had enough.

A letter by Thomas Brattle, a wealthy, Harvard-educated merchant and prestigious scientist, furthered Phipps's desire to take action. In a letter dated October 8, 1692, to an unknown correspondent—it began "Dear Rev Sir"—Brattle questioned the prosecution of witches. He did not understand how spectral evidence could be admitted. He pointed out the errors of the Salem judges in testing the witches, the bullying of the judges, the fact that the afflicted girls became hysterical only in the courtroom, and the fact that they never arrested any accused person related to themselves, such as Jonathan Corwin's mother-in-law. One of Brattle's strongest points was that some people who were accused had never even met the afflicted girls. Brattle then listed reputable men in England who agreed with his point of view and who also condemned the trials.

At last, many people were finally growing weary of bloodshed. It did not take long after this letter had been sent for Governor Phipps to write to the Privy Council in London, saying that he had forbidden any more imprisonment relating to witchcraft. On October 29, 1692, Phipps officially dissolved the Court of Oyer and Terminer.

The Witch Trials Memorial in Salem, Massachusetts, is made up of a stone wall and twenty granite benches engraved with the name of one of the accused.

Phipps replaced this court—made up of his friends William Stoughton, John Alden, Jonathan Corwin, John Hathorne, Nathaniel Ingerstoll, Bartholomew Gedney, Peter Sergeant, Samuel Sewall, and Walt Winthrop— with the new Superior Court of Judicature. The new court did not allow spectral evidence and condemned only three of fifty-six defendants. Phipps then pardoned those, along with others who were awaiting execution. In May 1693, Phipps set free any person accused of witchcraft that was still in jail.

After Samuel Parris was ousted from the parish, the new reverend, Joseph Green, tried to heal the torn community of Salem. Green reshuffled the seating plan of the parish, and the Putnams were seated next to the Nurses. In 1706, Green read the final apology from Ann Putnam Jr., who died, alone, in Salem Village at the age of thirty-seven.

In 1992, three hundred years after the trials and executions had occurred, the Salem Witch Trials Memorial, designed by James Cutler, was unveiled and honored in Salem. It is situated directly across from the site of the old meetinghouse.

Additionally, the November 2, 2001, issue of the *New York Times* published an article stating that "more than three centuries after they were accused, tried and hanged as unrepentant witches on Gallows Hill in Salem, Mass., five women have been officially exonerated by the state. The act, approved by Legislature, was signed on Halloween by the acting governor, cheering the descendants of Bridget Bishop, Susannah Martin, Alice Parker, Wilmott Redd, and Margaret Scott." Supposedly, the state had tried to follow through with this procedure in the past. In 1711, all of the accused were exonerated or their relatives were offered retribution. But perhaps because there was still such shame attached to the event, not all of the families came forward to accept this public apology. Then, in 1957, a state resolution cleared the name of one more victim, Ann Pudeator, and "certain other persons." (The 1957 resolution did not list specific names.) It was state representative Paul E. Tirone who helped push this act through. It stated that the "other persons" should be cleared by name. Tirone's wife, Sharon, was a descendant of Sarah Wildes, one of the accused women.

According to researchers Paul Boyer and Stephen Nissenbaum in *Salem Possessed: The Social Origins of Witchcraft*, "185 people were accused in Salem, 141 women and forty-four men. Of that number, fourteen women and five men were [hanged], the last group on September 22, 1692."

WHY WITCHCRAFT?

Today historians are still asking why this hysteria occurred at all. No one knows the exact answer, but someone is always studying new theories. Some suggest a condition known as conversion disorder, which was previously called hysteria. In conversion disorder, anxiety turns into physical signs, such as seizures. Such illnesses, as well as epilepsy, were hard to explain at the time and were therefore labeled as witchcraft. Among other explanations was the accidental consumption a fungus called ergot, which can grow on the grains residents of Salem would have been eating. Ergot can result in symptoms such as hallucinations and convulsions.

Other historians argue that the conflicts grew out of the rising merchant class in Salem Town. Possibly, the merchants stepped on the toes of the agricultural community to achieve more wealth and power, and the farmers retaliated. Several researchers believe the Putnam family fueled the accusations. Historian Richard Trask believes that the witch trials were nothing but a case of "clinical hysteria."

We may never know exactly what caused these girls to act out in these ways, throwing their communities into upheaval and chaos. But we can look at the facts and study history, learning from mistakes and moving forward.

TIMELINE

1609 Henry Hudson leads explorations in Massachusetts Bay.

1620 Pilgrims arrive in America on the *Mayflower* and establish Plymouth.

1626 The Naumkeag Indians occupy various sites in Massachusetts. Roger Conant establishes Salem as a trading post.

1629 Calvinist merchants, who simply want to reform, or "purify," the Calvinist church, establish the Massachusetts Bay Colony. A royal charter gives them a right to govern lands in what is present-day Massachusetts.

1630 John Winthrop is appointed the first governor and sails to Massachusetts.

1638 A small group of Puritans settle in what becomes known as Salem Village, five miles (eight kilometers) away from the center of town.

1649 In England, Charles I is executed.

1672 Salem Village acquires authority to begin a parish, hire a minister, and gather taxes for community improvements.

1689 Salem Village Church is formed, and Reverend Samuel Parris is ordained.

1692 In January, girls in Salem Village begin to exhibit strange physical "fits," and Doctor William Griggs concludes they are "bewitched." The girls are pressured to identify who is afflicting them.

1692 By February, magistrates Johnathan Hathorne and Jonathan Corwin have "examined" several of the accused, and the list of arrest warrants for other townspeople suspected of witchcraft rapidly increases.

1692 In May, Governor William Phipps sets up the special Court of Oyer and Terminer, "to hear and determine," to try the witchcraft cases.

1692 In June, Bridget Bishop is the first person to be found guilty of witchcraft and hanged on Gallows Hill. Through September, more than one hundred more individuals are accused and imprisoned.

1692 On October 29, as people of high-ranking stature are accused and spectral evidence becomes inadmissible during trials, Governor Phipps terminates the Court of Oyer and Terminer.

1696 One of the judges appointed to the Court of Oyer and Terminer, Samuel Sewall, publicly apologizes for his role in the trials and writes a proclamation for a day of fasting and penance by the government for its past sins.

1752 Salem Village changes its name to Danvers and is established as a separate district.

PAGE 23: EXCERPT FROM "EXECUTION OF REBECCA NURSE," JULY 19, 1692

(Warrant v. Rebecca Nurse)

To the Marshall of Essex or his deputie

There Being Complaint this day made (before us by Edward putnam and Jonathan putnam Yeomen both of Salem Village, Against Rebeca Nurce the wife of franc's Nurce of Salem Village for vehement Suspition, of haveing Committed Sundry acts of Witchcraft and thereby haveing donne Much hurt and Injury to the Bodys of Ann putnam the wife of Thomas putnam of Salem Village Anna puttnam the dauter of Said Thomas putnam and Abigail Williams &c You are therefore in theire Majesties names hereby required to apprehend and bring before us Rebeca Nurce the wife of franc's Nurce of Salem Village, to Morrow aboute Eight of the Clock in the forenoon at the house of Lt Nathaniell Ingersoll in Salem Village in order to her Examination Relateing to the aboves'd premises and hereof you are not to faile Salem March the 23'd 1691/2 p us *John. Hathorne] Assists *Jonathan Corwin] Assists

March 24'th 1691/2 I have apprehended the body of Rebeca Nurse and brought her to the house of Le't Nath. Ingersal where shee is in Costody

PAGE 41: PETITION FOR BAIL FROM ACCUSED WITCHES.

This petition is addressed to the governor and general assembly in Boston and was written by several women and men in jail. It is unknown who actually wrote the petition and some names are cut off at the end.

To the Honourable Governor and Councell and General Assembly now sitting at Boston: The humble petition of us whose names are subscribed here unto now prisoners at Ipswich humbly showeth that some of us have Lyen in the prison many months, and some of us many weekes, who are charged with Witchcraft, and not being conscious to our selves of any guilt of that nature Lying upon our consciences; our earnest request is that being the winter is so far come that we should be tried during this winter season, that we may be released out of prison for the present upon Bayle to answer what we are charged with in the Spring. For we are not in this unwilling nor afrayed to abide the tryall before any Judicature apoynted in convenient season of any crime of that nature; we hope you will put on the bonetts [?] of compassion so far as to consider of our suffering condition in the present state we are in, being likely to parish with cold in lying longer in prison in this cold season of the years, some of us being aged either about or near fourscore some though younger yet being with child, and one giving suck to a child not ten weeks old yet, and all of us weake and infirmed at the best and one fettered with woes half her years and all most distoyed with soe long an imprisonment. Thus hoping you will grant us a release at the present that we be not left to perish in this miserable condition we shall always pray.

Widow Penny, Widow Vincent, Widow Prince, Goodwife Greene of Havarell, the wife of Hugh Roe of Cape Anne, Mehitabel Downing, the Wife of Timothy Day, Goodwife Dicer of Piscataqua, Hanah Brumidge of Havarell, Rachel Hafield besides three or four men.

CONTEMPORARY ENGLISH TRANSLATION:

To the Honorable Governor, Council, and General Assembly now meeting in Boston: As stated in this humble petition from the Ipswich prisoners whose names are signed below, some of us have been imprisoned for many months, others for many weeks. We are all charged with witchcraft, but none of us knows what we've done to deserve this. Winter has now progressed so far that it's unlikely that we will be tried before the end of winter. Under these circumstances, we earnestly request that we be released on bail, to return in the spring to stand trial on these charges. We're not afraid to face trial on these charges before any court of justice that would be appointed at a convenient time. We hope you'll find it in your hearts to have pity on us in our present suffering. It is so terribly cold in the prison that we are in danger of dying from the cold. Some of us are almost eighty years old. Some of the younger women are pregnant. One woman gave birth less than ten weeks ago. All of us are weak and ill. One of us has been chained for six months and is almost dead from such a long imprisonment. We hope that you will grant us this temporary release and not leave us to die in such miserable conditions.

As always, we bow humbly before you.

Mrs. Penny, widowed. Mrs. Vincent, widowed. Mrs. Prince, widowed. Mrs Greene of Havarell. The wife of Hugh Roe of Cape Anne. Mehitabel Downing. The wife of Thimothy Day. Mrs. Dicer of Piscataqua. Hanah Brumidge of Havarell. Rachel Hafield. Also three or four men.

GLOSSARY

affliction The state of being in severe pain, either physical or mental.

apparition A supernatural appearance of a person or thing; a ghost.

charter A document issued by a sovereign state (a self-governing group), outlining the conditions under which a colony is organized and defining its rights.

coven An assembly of witches, especially of the number thirteen.

delusion The act of misleading.

deviate To differ from the normal.

doctrine Something, such as a belief, held and taught by a group, such as a church.

ergot poisoning Disease caused by a fungus in rye and other cereal grasses. Some believe that colonists who became sick with this disease would hallucinate and accuse people based on what they saw.

exonerate To clear from accusation of blame; to unburden.

Gallows Hill The rocky pasture surrounded by water that served as the scene of execution in Salem; also called Witch Hill.

heyday The period of one's greatest success.

immigrant A person who comes to a country to take up permanent residence.

magistrate A local official exercising administrative and often judicial functions.

manacle A shackle for hands; handcuffs.

mania Excitement; disorganization of behavior.

petition A formally drawn request bearing names of those who are asking a person or group in authority a favor.

Pilgrim A seventeenth-century Englishman or English-woman who believed in complete separation from the Church of England. Pilgrims settled in the colony of Plymouth.

poppet Earlier word for "puppet"; also an object made from hair and rags with pins sticking out of it, used as evidence of practicing witchcraft.

predestined Describes something that is decided or put in place prior to birth.

prosecutor A person who brings legal proceedings against another person, believing the accused is guilty of a crime.

Puritan A seventeenth-century Englishman or English-woman who wanted to "purify" the Church of England by removing all traces of associated Catholic items, such as crosses or vestments. Puritans settled in the Boston area around 1630 and absorbed the colony of Plymouth in 1692.

reprieve A temporary suspension of execution.

specter A visible spirit of terrifying nature.

spectral evidence Evidence accepted by the judges in the Salem courts meant to prove people's claims of spec-ters hurting them.

unrepentant Not showing sorrow or regret for misdeeds.

witch hunt The searching out and deliberate harassment of those (as political opponents) with unpopular views; a searching out for persecution those accused of witchcraft.

FOR MORE INFORMATION

Canadian Heritage Gallery
1326 Whiffletree Court
Mississauga, ON L5N 7R1
Canada
(905) 564-0067
Website: http://www.canadianheritage.org
The Canadian Heritage Gallery is home to "the most exten-
    sive collection of historical Canadiana on the Internet."

Historic Salem Incorporated
P.O. Box 865
Salem, MA 01970
(978) 745-0799
Website: http://historicsalem.org
Historic Salem Incorporated was founded in 1944 and
    strives to preserve the historic resources, such as sites
    and homes, of Salem, Massachusetts.

Massachusetts Archives
Secretary of the Commonwealth
220 Morrissey Boulevard
Boston, MA 02125
(617) 727-2816
Website: http://www.sec.state.ma.us/arc
The archives division of the Secretary of the Commonwealth
    preserves records and ensures they are accessible.

Massachusetts Historical Society
1154 Boylston Street
Boston, MA 02215
(617) 536-1608
Website: http://www.masshist.org

Founded in 1791, the Massachusetts Historical Society is an independent research library that is "particularly well-known for extensive holdings of personal papers from three presidents: John Adams, John Quincy Adams, and Thomas Jefferson."

Salem Witch Museum
19 ½ Washington Square North
Salem, MA 01970
(978) 744-1692
Website: http://www.salemwitchmuseum.com
The Salem Witch Museum brings its visitors right back to 1692 with "life-size stage sets, figures, lighting and a stirring narration. Live guides take you through changing interpretations of witches, the truth behind the stereotypes, witchcraft practice today and the frightening phenomenon of witch hunting."

University of Alberta
116 Street and 85 Avenue
Edmonton, AB T6G 2R3
Canada
Website: http://uofa.ualberta.ca
The University of Alberta's library is home to one of only four copies of Invectives Against the Sect of Waldensians, which describes "how to find, hunt, punish or even execute witches in Europe."

The Witch House
310 ½ Essex Street
Salem, MA 01970
(978) 744-8816
Website: http://www.salemweb.com/witchhouse

The Witch House was the home of judge Jonathan Corwin
and is the only remaining building from the time of the
Salem witch trials. Here visitors can experience what it
was like to live in 1692.

WEBSITES

Because of the changing nature of Internet links, Rosen
Publishing has developed an online list of websites related
to the subject of this book. This site is updated regularly.
Please use this link to access the list:

http://www.rosenlinks.com/UAH/Salem

FOR FURTHER READING

Fraustino, Lisa Rowe. *Dear America: I Walk in Dread.* New York, NY: Scholastic, 2011.

Hill, Frances. *A Delusion of Satan: The Full Story of the Salem Witch Trials.* Cambridge, MA: Da Capo Press, 2002.

Knudsen, Shannon. *Alice Ray and the Salem Witch Trials.* Brookfield, CT: Millbrook, 2011.

Marciniak, Kristin. *The Salem Witch Trials* (Perspectives Library). North Mankato, MN: Cherry Lake, 2014.

Mather, Cotton. *On Witchcraft.* New York, NY: Peter Pauper Press, 1950.

Schanzer, Rosalyn. *Witches: The Absolutely True Tale of Disaster in Salem.* Washington, DC: National Geographic, 2011.

Thompson, Paul B. *The Devil's Door: A Salem Witchcraft Story.* Berkley Heights, NJ: Enslow, 2010.

Trask, Richard B. *The Devil Hath Been Raised: A Documentary History of the Salem Village Witchcraft Outbreak of March 1692.* Cambridge, MA: Yeoman Press, 1997.

Waxman, Laura Hamilton. *Who Were the Accused Witches of Salem? And Other Questions About the Witchcraft Trials.* Minneapolis, MN: Lerner, 2012.

Yolen, Jane. *The Salem Witch Trials: An Unsolved Mystery from History.* Cambridge, MA: Audible Audiobook, 2013.

BIBLIOGRAPHY

Boyer, Paul, and Stephen Nissenbaum. *Salem Possessed: The Social Origins of Witchcraft.* Cambridge, MA: Harvard University Press, 1974.

Cahill, Robert Ellis. *The Horrors of Salem's Witch Dungeon* (Collectible Classics No. 9). Peabody, MA: Old Salt Box Publishing Co., 1986.

Discovery Education. "Salem Witch Trials: The World Behind the Hysteria." Retrieved November 10, 2014 (http://school.discoveryeducation.com/ schooladventures/salemwitchtrials).

Hayoun, Massoud. "For the Roots of Salem Witch Hysteria, Look at the Next Town Over." October 28, 2014. Aljazeera America. Retrieved November 10, 2014 (http://america.aljazeera.com/ articles/2014/10/28/for-the-roots -ofsalemwitchhysterialookthenexttownover.html).

Hill, Frances. *A Delusion of Satan: The Full Story of the Salem Witch Trials.* Cambridge, MA: Da Capo Press, 1997.

Hill, Frances. *The Salem Witch Trials Reader.* Cambridge, MA: Da Capo Press, 2000.

Karlsen, Carol F. *The Devil in the Shape of a Woman: Witchcraft in Colonial New England.* New York, NY: W. & W. Norton and Company, 1988.

Kramer, Heinrich, and James Sprenger. *The Malleus Malificarum.* Mineola, NY: Dover Publications Inc., 1971.

Linder, Douglas. "An Account of Events in Salem." University of Missouri. September 2009. Retrieved November 10, 2014 (http://law2.umkc.edu/faculty/ projects/ftrials/salem/asa_hob.htm).

The Mather Papers. *Massachusetts Historical Society Collections*, 4th Sermon, Vol. 8. Boston, 1912.

New York Times. "Massachusetts Clears 5 from Salem Witch Trials." *National Report*, November 2, 2001, p. A12.

Robinson, Enders A. *The Devil Discovered: Salem Witch-craft, 1692.* Prospect Heights, IL: Waveland Press, 2001.

Sewall, Samuel. *Diary.* Massachusetts Historical Society Collections, 5th Sermon, Vols. 1–3. Boston, 1918.

Trask, Richard B. *The Devil Hath Been Raised: A Documentary History of the Salem Village Witchcraft Outbreak of March 1692.* Cambridge, MA: Yeoman Press, 1997.

INDEX

ABOUT THE AUTHORS

Zoe Lowery is an editor and writer living in Colorado. When she's not investigating local and American history, she likes trying out unusual ice cream flavor combinations.

Jennifer MacBain-Stephens is also the author of *Women's Suffrage: Giving the Right to Vote to All Americans* and *Gertrude Elion: Nobel Prize Winner in Physiology and Medicine*, as well as three books of poetry. She lives in the Washington, D.C., area with her family.

PHOTO CREDITS

Cover MPI/Archive Photos/Getty Images; p. 3 Lone Wolf Photography/Shutterstock.com; pp. 4–5 (background) Enigmangels/Shutterstock.com; pp. 5 (inset), 23 Salem Witch Trials Documentary Archive and Transcription Project, University of Virginia, http://salem.lib.virginia.edu; pp. 6, 12, 19 (background), 21, 26, 33, 40, 44 (background), Ellina Litmanovich; pp. 8, 39 Private Collection/Peter Newark American Pictures/Bridgeman Images; p. 9 © North Wind Picture Archives; p. 13 © Massachusetts Historical Society, Boston, MA, USA/Bridgeman Images; p. 17 © Maurice Savage/Alamy; pp. 19 (inset), 36 © Peabody Essex Museum, Salem, Massachusetts, USA/Bridgeman Images; p. 27 Raymond Forbes/SuperStock; p. 28 Library of Congress Prints and Photographs Division; p. 31 Kean Collection/Archive Photos/Getty Images; p. 34 © North Wind Picture Archives/The Image Works; p. 41 Library of Congress Manuscript Division; p. 42 Hulton Archive/Getty Images; p. 44 (inset) Collections of the Maine State Museum; p. 45 © AP Images; cover, p. 1 design elements Piotr Krzeslak/Shutterstock.com (flag), Aleksandrs Bondars/Shutterstock.com (scroll); cover and interior pages background textures chudo-yudo/Shutterstock.com, Alina G/Shutterstock.com, Attitude/Shutterstock.com, sl_photo/Shutterstock.com

Designer: Michael Moy; Editor: Heather Moore Niver